Visit

INDEPENDENCE HALL

By Alexander Wood

Gareth Stevens
Publishing

Please visit our website, www.garethstevens.com. For a free color catalog of all our high-quality books, call toll free 1-800-542-2595 or fax 1-877-542-2596.

Library of Congress Cataloging-in-Publication Data

Wood, Alexander, 1978-
Visit Independence Hall / Alexander Wood.
    p. cm. — (Landmarks of liberty)
Includes index.
ISBN 978-1-4339-6386-5 (pbk.)
ISBN 978-1-4339-6387-2 (6-pack)
ISBN 978-1-4339-6384-1 (library binding)
1. Independence Hall (Philadelphia, Pa.)—Juvenile literature. 2. United States—Politics and government—1775-1783—Juvenile literature. 3. United States—Politics and government—1783-1789—Juvenile literature. 4. Philadelphia (Pa.)—Buildings, structures, etc.—Juvenile literature. I. Title.
F158.8.I3W66 2012
973.3'13—dc23
                              2011019302

First Edition

Published in 2012 by
Gareth Stevens Publishing
111 East 14th Street, Suite 349
New York, NY 10003

Copyright © 2012 Gareth Stevens Publishing

Designer: Andrea Davison-Bartolotta
Editor: Therese Shea

Photo credits: Cover, back cover (all), (pp. 2-3, 21, 22-23, 24 flag background), (pp. 4-21 corkboard background), pp. 1, 4, 5, 13 Shutterstock.com; p. 7 Stock Montage/Getty Images; p. 9 DC Productions/Valueline/Thinkstock; p. 11 Buyenlarge/Getty Images; p. 15 SuperStock/Getty Images; p. 17 MPI/Getty Images; p. 19 Richard Cummins/Lonely Planet Images/Getty Images; p. 20 Harry Hamburg/NY Daily News Archive/Getty Images.

Printed in the United States of America

CPSIA compliance information: Batch #CW12GS: For further information contact Gareth Stevens, New York, New York at 1-800-542-2595.

Contents

Words in the glossary appear in **bold** type the first time they are used in the text.

Philadelphia's Famous Hall

Have you ever visited Philadelphia, Pennsylvania? It's a city with a lot of history! It was an important place during the American colonies' fight for independence from England. The Founding Fathers met in Philadelphia to make decisions about the war and about the new nation. They met in a building that still stands. Today, it's one of the most famous buildings in the United States. Because of its importance during the American **Revolution**, this building is now called Independence Hall.

Tell Me More!

The city of Philadelphia was founded by William Penn in 1682.

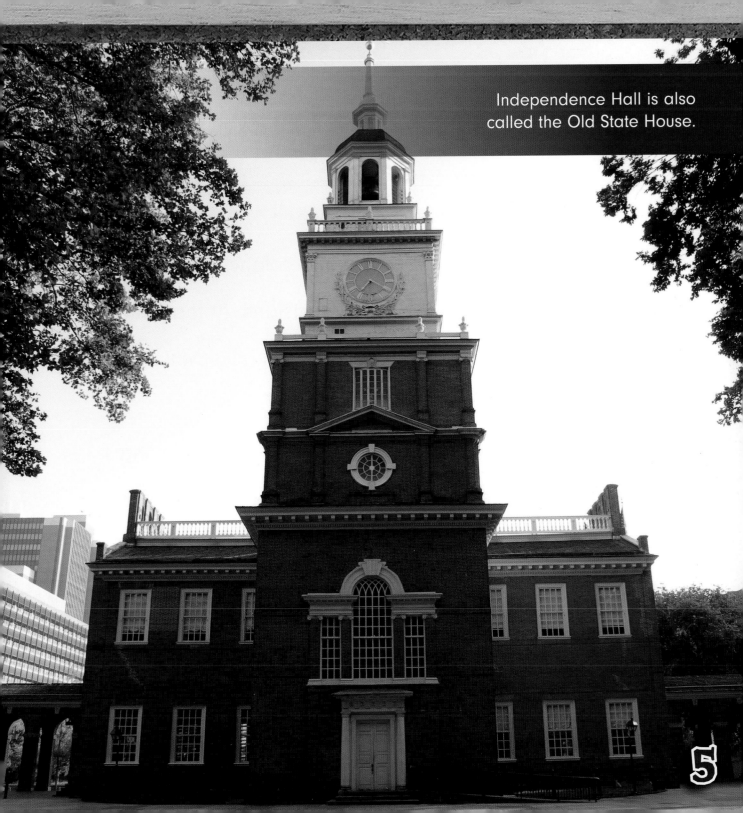

Independence Hall is also called the Old State House.

Beginnings

Independence Hall was built between 1732 and 1756. It was the state house of the Pennsylvania colony. A state house is where lawmakers gather to make decisions. At that time, American colonists made some of their own laws while England made others.

By the 1770s, many colonial leaders were questioning whether they should be ruled by England at all. England was passing laws they didn't like and forcing taxes on the colonies. Many colonists became angry. They wanted more say in how they were governed.

This picture of Independence Hall in the 1770s shows Philadelphia during the time of the American Revolution.

7

The Second Continental Congress

On May 10, 1775, colonial leaders gathered in the **assembly** room of the Pennsylvania State House. They formed the Second Continental Congress. This group made decisions about the future of the American colonies.

One of the first decisions was to form the Continental army to fight the British. Congress named George Washington from the Virginia colony as the army's commander in chief. On July 4, 1776, Congress approved the Declaration of Independence. This **document** announced that the colonies governed themselves.

Tell Me More!

Many believe that the state house bell rang on July 8 to mark the first public reading of the Declaration of Independence. This bell is called the Liberty Bell.

The Declaration of Independence was signed in Independence Hall. The bottle of ink and the quill pens used for the signing are still there.

9

The War for Independence

England didn't want to let go of the colonies. Many battles were fought during the American Revolution. The capture of Philadelphia was one goal of the British forces. At times, the Second Continental Congress moved the location of their **sessions** to avoid danger. They held a session in Baltimore, Maryland, for 3 months before going back to Philadelphia.

From September 1777 to June 1778, Philadelphia was occupied by the British. During that time, Congress met in other towns in Pennsylvania.

Tell Me More!

In 1777, the Second Continental Congress met in the assembly room of the Pennsylvania State House and approved the design of the US flag.

The Americans hoped the Battle of Germantown in 1777, shown here, would help them recapture Philadelphia from the British. However, the Continental army lost and withdrew their forces.

11

The Constitutional Convention

The first US **constitution**, called the Articles of Confederation, was **ratified** and became law in 1781. It didn't give the central government much power. States didn't have to follow the central government's laws or pay taxes to it. The weak central government made the young country weak.

In 1787, another meeting took place at the Pennsylvania State House. This meeting was called the Constitutional Convention. Over 4 months, state **representatives** created a new plan for the US government.

Tell Me More!

In 1778, British troops used the chairs and tables of the Pennsylvania State House as firewood. Most of the furniture there today was made to look like the originals.

As the Constitutional Convention's president, George Washington sat at a desk in the front of the assembly room. His chair is still in Independence Hall.

The US Constitution

The new US Constitution balanced power between the states and the central government. The plan included a president, a court system, and a **legislature** divided into two parts, or houses. Each state would elect representatives to the new legislature.

Members of the Constitutional Convention approved the Constitution on September 17, 1787. Next, copies were sent to state legislatures for approval. In 1788, enough states ratified the Constitution to make it law. An original **draft** is still located in the west **wing** of the state house.

George Washington, dressed in black, addresses the members of the Constitutional Convention as its president.

A New Name

The role of the Pennsylvania State House in the founding of the nation was forgotten for a time. Then, in 1824, the Marquis de Lafayette visited Philadelphia. Lafayette was a French general who had helped the United States win the American Revolution. The state house was redecorated for his visit. The assembly room was renamed the "Hall of Independence."

The Hall of Independence was used for important visitors after that. In the 1850s, the entire building was called Independence Hall for the first time.

Tell Me More!

In 1865, the body of President Abraham Lincoln was laid in the assembly room of Independence Hall for a time after his death.

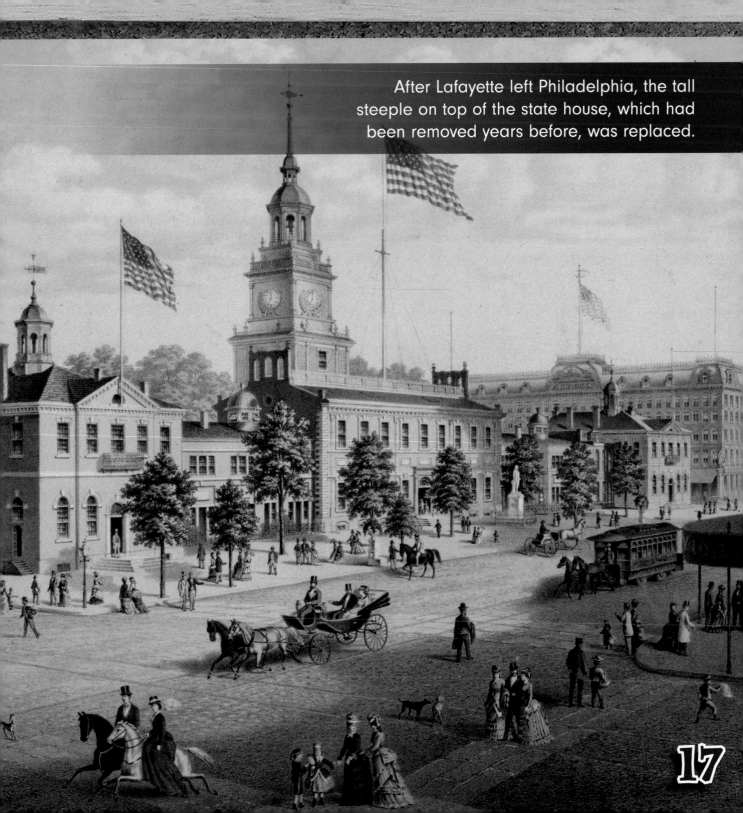

After Lafayette left Philadelphia, the tall steeple on top of the state house, which had been removed years before, was replaced.

17

Independence National Historical Park

In 1951, Independence Hall and the surrounding three blocks were given to the National Park Service. The building and the land became Independence National Historical Park. It's set aside so that people from Philadelphia, the United States, and all over the world can visit the birthplace of the country's independence.

Independence Hall has been made to look as it did during the Constitutional Convention. People can take tours, see the Liberty Bell, and walk the grounds as the Founding Fathers did over 200 years ago.

Tell Me More!

More than 200 people work at Independence National Historical Park. Over 150 more volunteers give tours to visitors.

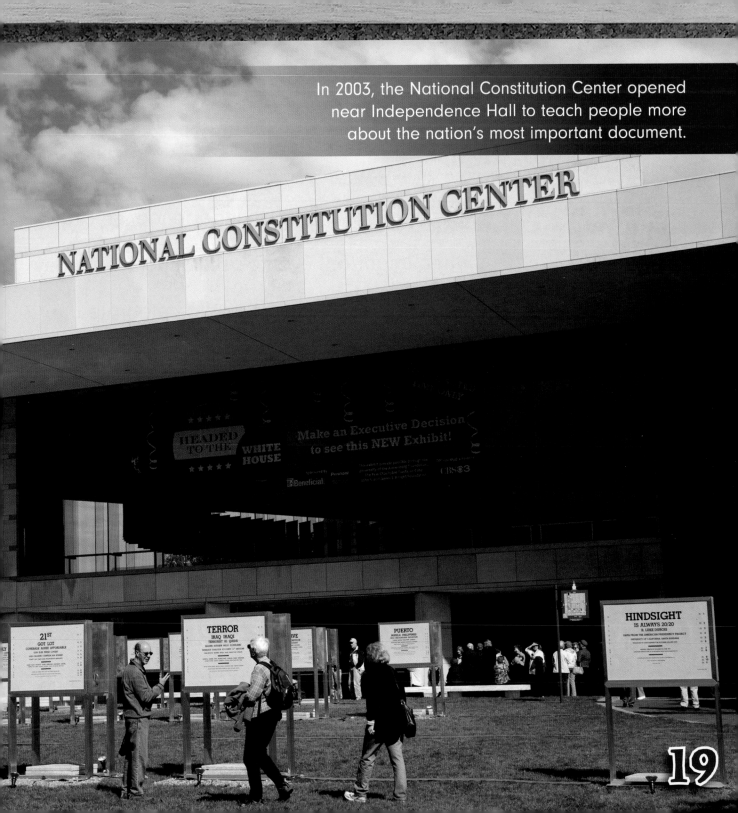

In 2003, the National Constitution Center opened near Independence Hall to teach people more about the nation's most important document.

19

History Still Happens Here

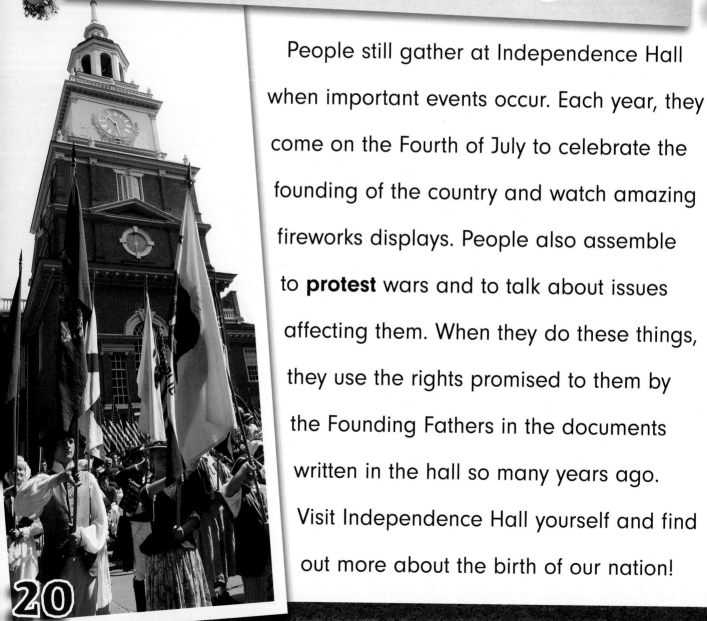

People still gather at Independence Hall when important events occur. Each year, they come on the Fourth of July to celebrate the founding of the country and watch amazing fireworks displays. People also assemble to **protest** wars and to talk about issues affecting them. When they do these things, they use the rights promised to them by the Founding Fathers in the documents written in the hall so many years ago. Visit Independence Hall yourself and find out more about the birth of our nation!

More About Independence Hall

Location:
Chestnut Street, between 5th & 6th Streets, Philadelphia, Pennsylvania

Built:
1732–1756

Why It's Important:
It's the place where the Declaration of Independence and US Constitution were written.

Fun Fact:
The basement was once Philadelphia's dog pound!

Cost to Tour Hall:
Free

Glossary

assembly: people gathered for a common purpose

constitution: the basic laws by which a country or state is governed

design: the pattern or shape of something

document: a formal piece of writing

draft: a document before completion

legislature: a body of lawmakers

protest: to strongly oppose something

ratify: to approve

representative: a member of a lawmaking body who acts for voters

revolution: the overthrow of a government

session: a meeting of an official group

volunteer: one who works without pay

wing: a part of a building that sticks out from the main part

For More Information

Books

Schaefer, Ted, and Lola M. Schaefer. *Independence Hall*. Chicago, IL: Heinemann Library, 2006.

Staton, Hilarie. *Independence Hall*. New York, NY: Chelsea Clubhouse, 2010.

Websites

Independence Hall
www.ushistory.org/tour/independence-hall.htm
Read more facts about Independence Hall and the changes it has undergone over the years.

Independence Hall
www.nps.gov/inde/independence-hall-1.htm
See up-close photos of the objects used by the Founding Fathers in the creation of the Declaration of Independence and the US Constitution.

Independence National Historical Park
www.cr.nps.gov/history/online_books/hh/17/hh17g.htm
Learn more about how Independence Hall was restored and the many people who made this possible.

Index